Free Verse Editions
Edited by Jon Thompson

INTERGLACIAL

Tracy Zeman

Parlor Press
Anderson, South Carolina
www.parlorpress.com

Parlor Press LLC, Anderson, South Carolina, 29621

© 2026 by Parlor Press
All rights reserved.
Printed in the United States of America
S A N: 2 5 4 - 8 8 7 9

Library of Congress Cataloging-in-Publication Data

Names: Zeman, Tracy author
Title: Interglacial / Tracy Zeman.
Description: Anderson, South Carolina : Parlor Press, 2026. | Series: Free
  verse editions | Summary: "In lyric language spliced with borrowed text
  and single-sharp moments, Interglacial connects a changing region to our
  deep past and near future. Of bird, rock, and lake, this travelogue
  catalogs species and places"-- Provided by publisher.
Identifiers: LCCN 2025049493 (print) | LCCN 2025049494 (ebook) | ISBN
  9781643175539 paperback | ISBN 9781643175546 adobe pdf | ISBN
  9781643175553 epub
Classification: LCC PR? (print) | LCC PR? (ebook)
LC record available at https://lccn.loc.gov/2025049493
LC ebook record available at https://lccn.loc.gov/2025049494

2 3 4 5

Cover image: "Night Moraine" by Elizabeth Claire Rose. © Tracy Zeman.
  Used by permission.
Book design by David Blakesley.

Parlor Press, LLC is an independent publisher of scholarly and trade titles in
print and multimedia formats. This book is available in paperback and ebook
formats from Parlor Press on the World Wide Web at https://www.parlorpress.
com or through online and brick-and-mortar bookstores. For submission
information or to find out about Parlor Press publications, write to Parlor
Press, 3015 Brackenberry Drive, Anderson, South Carolina, 29621, or email
editor@parlorpress.com.

For Matt, Lucy, & Katie
& in memory of Kathy Zeman, 1952–2015

Contents

Interglacial

This world of the Lake

— Lorine Niedecker
"Lake Superior"

~

NORTH

Sand cliffs at Sleeping Bear Point
as we search for stones   daughter wants to keep them
silt memorial   compass sediment   *long dead trunks*
of ancient cedars washed on shore on pitch & ghost forest
we try to see across the long blue
our feet wet at the edge of a new country

>   beach pea
>   *of the sea*

Early spring   common mergansers on the pond
first migrant yellow-rumps & bluebirds
traverse foredunes & back dunes scattered
by blowouts of barren sand eroded by wind
the smell of the lake follows me inland
wood-smoke & spruce supreme

>   embers cool
>   to dark

Lighthouse shadow divides the bay in two
cormorants dive from the water's surface
webbed feet propelling them   to the depths
where the dead go   waves clamoring
up the rock-face   an uncontrolled experiment
of *scale & intensity* we've never known

      sweet seas
      foam flecked

      ~

Daughter makes up a song
as she watches the ship recede from shore
lit as brightly as a small city   we camp on the sands
on that same wind   orange tent starred
against brink   mile-thick ice-sheets fracture slate
& bedrock   leave dune & drift in their wake

      coral-body
      sea into stone

Shale shaped by water into river valleys
my canoe seemed as if it hung suspended
in that element   rough-hewn forts built by fur-traders
& black robes   longboats portaging
smooth gray & pink undulated rocks whirl up
to the forest surface   Precambrian remnants

      gneiss shot
      with granite

      ~

Black-capped chickadee's two-tone whistle
in early morning   call it *creative destruction*   or
the power of our bodies   so that we alone can live here
in fear of the still places   night descends
in *waves of black water*   the *drift & slip*
of a body   pale necks stretched in flight

      wingsnap
      over tamarack

SPRING

Marsh wren weaves a small ball-shaped nest
from dry grass   silver carp roots out aquatic
plants & stirs sediment   disturbing the breeding grounds
in the rivers surrounding   spring comes
under snowcover   gilded leaves
rhizomatic tendrils   *form   frond*
finch   fur   common reed   wormwood
trees transpiring water make blue from molten rock
her body outside the shower in morning
steam stippled on glass

       Little La Cloche Island
       harbors mouse
                & vole

I watch an Iceland gull glide between smokestacks
near Celeron Island   star-shapes in ice-melt
red-tagged red-wings   earlier this year
ever darker territory   two downy woodpeckers
bounce branch to branch   pattern of
ice ages from slight changes
in Earth's orbit   sawtooth fluctuation
becomes a continuum   becomes permanent putting off
flicker careens across boardwalk
wing-print on ice

    olive finch undulates
    alder
         for aphid

~

Sun's luminosity increasing slowly over time
thinking the natural & social worlds together
small flock of turkeys   pipe stem adorned
with the head of an ivory-billed woodpecker
war filling every depression   in our *knowledge of*
the material world survive fragments   light
lake-sheen   late-season goldfinches
their cupped nests holding rainwater   after summer
white-footed mouse   red squirrel
trouble structures with young & seed

   milkweed bark
   & thistle-down
      make home

   ~

Ice crunch under boot   geese honking above
she had questions about *home* & what might be revealed
a sense of things about to *crack open*
invention & conceit & whose journey
turkey vultures arriving for summer
before redpolls fly north to arctic nesting grounds
crossing of seasons   *a beaver & a feather*
for the forest   a detour between two presences
daughter knows time & tides   dog returns
as I call her name into the dry grass

          chickadee probes cattail
          for shy-cosmet
                         larva

The biological origins for moral reasoning
floating islands of fur-bearing boats
after extermination in Europe   hair-shafts
locked together with barbs   pounded into felt
for rich & poor alike   wardrobe record
process of dying   only the deepest
forests   & then an unmaking
sluice   trade   iron-kettle   river
Fish & Furres   words like chromosomes
interlocked in cause & effect

    beaver-skiff
    on oxbow
            & moon-glow

    ~

At the last *a natural interruption of the natural sequence*
in dreams we feel *unexpected affinities*
tap the ice & watch a line race through the thin mantle
dog's paws pounding a packed trail
robin's return signals the junco's departure
succession of frost on moss on stone
frozen pools thawing for spring frogs
an original system   continuous foil of transformations
downies seeking mates create perfect circles
in dead trunks   a matching of shapes

        mallards float
        down River Rouge's
                        black ink

POINTE MOUILLEE

I wake early & in all that black   leave home
moisture in the air made visible by clouds   blue coolness
rogue waves borrowing form from the troposphere
harlequin in flight   floating world of coots canvasbacks
& hooded mergansers   white moon ringed with black
we peddle the rocky berm counting ducks

census of species in a long series of signs

            daughter's stars thinly inked
she sings while she draws   cattail   tree swallow
song sparrow's burnt streaks a sunburst from beak to chest
like the cumulus along the lake's perimeter
drifting & flattening into nothing into
a smooth white haze

Pied-billed grebes swim around semi-submerged barrels
signpost grackle shimmers   purple & black
lake as chemical reservoir   water over shoal over sandbar over
the tern's silver wing-tips   I have said nothing of the muskrats
swimming the lagoon   their rat-tails surfacing
as they sink between impoundments

every formal experiment is a move away

                    narrative in new rock   no jaws no teeth
only *expanded temporalities*   sea lampreys in Lake Ontario
for a century before descending into Erie
little more than   a *leathery cartilaginous tube & digestive track*
confused seas divided into units   we run to the shore
use my boot as touch-stone

~

Thinking across scales   issues of agency taken up
in an *age of limits* & dull absence   the lakes tip
one into another   long billed black-bellied dunlins
amble mudflat for mollusks   we collect the names
like specimens   hoarding them while we can
tributary leavetakers & new arrivals braided into

an endless dark corridor

                    into pearl-rush then button harvest for
mother-of-pearl   *a heart a foot & two hinged shells*
empty niche   for zebra & quagga to occupy
the shallows & the depths   swamp-rose mallow
spiny softshell turtle   *in a time-scale relevant*   we watch
a yellow-headed blackbird out of range   sing

MIGRATION

Eastern towhee scratches dead leaves
black-headed & rusty-flanked   a white cloud
late snow thaws as spotted cabbage flowers
twist up & break through   singing
its name from a low perch   phoebe flicks
its tail   spring-hinge voyager

      a foil
      for this

Cold April morning I descend
a small bridge over wet   dark-shaded
swamp sparrow   deep chestnut   singular
occupant   heart-leafed marsh marigold emergent
with early butterflies seeking ellipsoidal streams
inaccessible to us   rendering life

      a scaled
      diagram

Onoclea sensiblis spores on deep red stems
will die off at slightest frost in autumn   blue-gray
gnatcatcher still enough for me to notice
white eye-ring   *the work of living*
field of transformation of treading &
tinder   of a *cumulative resonance*

      of counter-
      course

Pearl-shaped tick near the white-throated
sparrow's right eye   *unflinching*
us out of ourselves   shuffling forward & back
claws etching leaf-litter   circle of
not-yet-morning bird chatter
in deep blue   I shift my making to

      tread
      sight

Catbird's strange warbles & sequences
a question follows the final rising note
red-breasted nuthatches needle Point Pelee's
dwarfed red cedars   warblers low in brush
peek orange or yellow   magnolia & bay-breasted
ingest pebbles   gizzard grit

      sand's
      end

Limbs pounded small by water
sand & sand & sand   masked common yellow-
throat & chestnut-sided   Solomon's seal
the jack's single-folded petal shielding
puddled dutchman's breeches   delicate
dispel   little known dreams & barrens

      in molecular
      machinery

Cabin-memory in the woods on the shore
of this lake or another   ocean ghost
crowd gathers to glimpse a Kentucky warbler
alive   black crescent beneath eyes
sumac & clammy weed   wind-blown
heedless denial   shallow sands

      down-
      bound

Belief in registers   here trees leaf out later
in Lake Erie's coolness
blue currents   blue ash & black walnut
an exercise in focused awareness   scarlet tanager
orchard oriole orbit   fallout after night flight
black-throated blue & black-throated green

      compass
      knot

~

RABBIT BAY

At the shoreline the cottage stays cool
long into summer   Superior engulfing the heat
into its deep   sunlight with last winter inside it
one world leading into another   the beginning
of something all-human   lake-memory
peninsula-bound   we walk out to the bay
a notch in the Keweenaw   a portage
to be made   sea-shape cut
into the green of sunlight on wave

      a fevered state
      between glaciers

Fog settles like *sea distance* or *sunrise*
north of Superior a circumpolar boreal forest
from *Boreas*   northwind   sphagnum bogs &
black pine   balsam poplar a specialist
in disturbed soil   light loosened from windthrow
watch the brown creeper trace a line
ascending to the top & then starting over
in an act of becoming   daughter collects
stones for her windowsill

      sandcliff
      into quarry

A box turtle shell on our path
yellow-green stars etched-lines & raised mounds
northern white cedars & mooseberry
wood-bound carapace   our own animal feelings
unmade as resource   or inland sea
part of an underlying conglomerate
propagating one body as dominant
we pedal toward sand & wave
gray jays quiet in spruce & jack

     bind nest
     with spider silk

Huddled on the screened porch
we watch the lake at dusk
steam from the small sauna
escapes the roof in wisps   black-backed
woodpecker alights deadwood   follows
beetles through the burned forest
ephemeral & repeating   a pattern
our soft talking makes   elemental & briefly
fixed   from continental rift

     redstone
     by wave

UPPER PENINSULA

Fayette ghost   company town
at earth-end limestone & dolomite cliffs
smelt ore into pig iron   slag
heaped beneath laborers' quarters
behind metalsmith & carpenter
kilns open skyward
now   *structures of perception*
Garden Peninsula tapers to fish-
town to second growth hardwood
after charcoal cuttings
stratifications of both kinds   snail curl
harbor   what word
was used to raze   I was

under a mosquito sky

Canoeing the Manistique River
breeding sites rife
after another wet spring
puddles & warms
swarm over us   jacket cover
through Seney swerve
orders of civilization
constructed system construes
angry goose trails
our wake   protecting
goslings   indigo bunting

flashes bright
from bank   *intelligible mark*

skin raised red

At Scott Point   hundreds
of Canadian swallowtails blanket
sand   dorsal-baskers
tide-pool flutter   *sustained*
project   black roots broken white
shells   lyre-leaved-rock-cress
pollen-float   clusters of fire-stained
stones   hearth-remainder
agency in the context
drive back on Gould City Road
two sandhill cranes edge
a readymix plant   we stop
to watch   primary   producer

SUPERIOR

By what measure a ship mast
pine-hunger   interlaced canopies
continuous ceiling of needles
oak-incubator   river-shelter   dark corridor
the *age of pine* floated downriver
after the clear cutting   *a service on the surface*
railroads to the interior abandoned &
rails sold for scrap   a measure of man
a spawning fish   soil ash ingot
some increased output   the cool
surrounding me

      winter wren
      haunts
      rotting wood

Lichen composite of algae & fungi
long draping stems falling
from black spruce   shingled-rock-shield
on outcrop   as I come I am
& I keep repeating   sphagnum moss as engine
as coral on land as coal as bog   a slow
conversion   I had to return when the sand
grew cold in autumn   wood-stove
burning a lake-song   midden
of beached pine cones at house's edge
dog's tail a rudder in water as she retrieves

      conifer's dark mass
      tan wings
      black masks

     ~

Her little scrawl at the edge of my notebook
while I am away   watching brown waves
crash against cold beach   single horned lark
shuffling   golden leaves pooling like fish
on the icy surface   breeding storms rain & fog
like the sea   a head lake   crust of granite
firedot   an *experiment with beginning*
with *wave-worn edges*   alluvial fans
& damp depressions   beach of sandstone
river gravel at the end & chickadees
roving through dwarfed crowns

     horseshoe harbor
     stunted trees
     bedrock rift

The modern state   a bias toward
continuity toward   moss-grown stones
& cliffs of stacked rock   old concrete dock paralleled
by boulders & railroad ties   our own invention
we're forced to live within   the rest
treated as curiosities   identity as nexus   *the snow*
crusted & the deer breaking through became trapped
hunters walked up to them & cut their throats
with knives   wind & rain slashing
when I arrived   waves pushing wrack
you revel in brokenness   claim catastrophe claim

pine needle
on window
lake edge rumble

~

A deer dead for five days
a red stone calumet   I canoe the edge
first beach then rock layered striations
wave-wet   horsehair lichen   white cedar
crevice-grown   yarrow on cliff edge   make coherence
from shatter   received from sun from crude forts
& fisheries   bring sturgeon in spring
& herring in fall   *series of contingencies*   boil water
from fire-heated stone   winter becomes staggered
becomes a time of engulfed by waves
red squirrel's *tchick tchick tchick* as I pass beneath

    whorl-sifted snow
    white pine
    canopy

KEWEENAW

Stars when I fetch wood in early morning
scrape ash from stove   begin again
one flat red rock in my pocket   single herring gull
on still lake   beach-wall of half-submerged metal barrels
painted & filled with black jagged rock   rock shaped bone
bone ground to sand   *drive a boat aground the rocky shoals*
steel-blade iron-kettle flintlock-rifle rum   melted snow
on leaves beads into domes into *tattered gray clouds*

     canots du nord
     carry dark pelts

Glowing island outside my window   *manitou Mitsipe*
the sway that comes from nothing   clusters of hunters in winter
become a time of particular horror   famine root grub frozen
marshland   precariousness of corn   crowded in refugee cities
common enemy   common ally   mining veins of copper
on Isle Royale with stone hammers   canoes swallowed
by waves or split open on rock   climb the boat's rigging
to flee bitter water & freeze to death there

     beaver harvest
     bark & aspen bud

Unequal distribution of costs   in *the smoke & the spoil*
I trek up a dirt-graded road   juncos & tree sparrows scatter
dog underfoot on the way to summit   golden-crowned
kinglets chittering in branches   a concentric mass
stromatolites & their calcareous bodies   red-breasted nuthatch
high & small   ash like cells   *watch ourselves cross*
the dark   dog retrieves two bones   small skull & another
children of the Holocene   some radioactivity in the register

      atlatl from sea
      & wood

      ~

A peculiar biological form of negativity   my dark word horde
a secluded beach down a two-track   impassable ruts & *bare wastes*
of great extent   sluiceways & holding ponds   aquatic-buckbean
velvetleaf   winterberry   old red dog in road barks a warning
a living substrate   I back away from the steep overhang
tamarack from *akemantak*   snowshoe wood
dense & resinous   how to have this destruction
call themselves *dwellers of the peninsula*   small sea inside

      shore scalloped
      in vaulted coves

Olive-sided flycatcher   rusty blackbird   lesser scaups
genetic relics   increased selenium from copper refining
a metalloid byproduct   recorded in *I thought*
I would know   & black to the top with spruce
lake-sun   dog asleep by fire after frigid swim
boots drying   evening on beach after autumn mountain climb
after word after corresponding is not anymore
to be found repeating in the wood bone lake sand skin

      ash-heap
      behind shed

      ~

Engine of human selection   gray-cheeked thrush on bramble log road
our innermost & long ago   convergent narratives
in the *black pocket of memory*   velocity of infraction
inability to disperse   rhyolite bluff descent through fault gorge
bottleneck   biotic contraction   afterlife of organisms
pursued until   sun through low clouds   white rafts of surf-foam
like the shadow-species still wandering who will pay down
the extinction debt   *identity as a series of moral linkages*

      in glacial ice
      & tree-ring

Rusty cliff ferns & ruffed grouse in woods as we ascend
a world in miniature on Mt Baldy   craggy rock &
woodland pinedrops   maidenhair spleenwort   DNA stores
hurtling waves   canoe covered in yellow bird rind
sewn with fine conifer roots   canoeman voyageur mutiny
some drowning   netting fish as they *glide between Rocks*
seines & hook-lines   remedial plan for the canalization
of St Mary's River   phenols ammonia & PAHs

    Epoufette Bay
    two coopers once

    ⁓

Copper-rush ghost towns & stamp-plant leftovers
Red Jacket Calumet   clintonia baneberry heart-leafed arnica
deep-shaft mines 9,000 feet down   solitary marten
hunts red-backed voles beneath snow-covered spaces
carbon-store   sand sand   *sometimes a bird*
sometimes a stone   the horned lark's black necklace
crush to recover fine granules &
refine again   *water that touched shore so long ago*

    elements leach
    into green-star stone

SEA

Skeletons & sunken
impressions burrows tracks
correlating with rock sequences
graptolites in deepwater
shales & shallow limestones
as films of carbon
on bedding planes   the delta

heaped in thin

severances   as field
of history   as the sea
transgressed & regressed
over land bare & pitted
slain marked O   here we
subsume continents &
drift copper   blanketlike

bodies found in

conglomerates
barbarous echo dust
carried southward by glaciers
will you   some silver
found within   gaps
where the sea withdrew

brachiopod shell into

shoal   only
a short time
from narrative & primitive
lungs   words &
things   small units
built up century
over century   knower &
known

wrapped in ongoing

reconfigurations of the world
a performative accounting
my body & yours
a hard record
ice flowing under
its own weight leaves
an apron

of outwash

~

THEANO POINT

We start by walking

forested crescent bay rising to steep Precambrian peninsula
of pitchblende
                        & granite
                        cut by diabase dikes

fractured & mineralized with pink-calcite chlorite & hematite

sand & cobble beach below

rocks sorted into piles of similar size by waves
some places persist from their beginnings
some cruelty escapes without our wanting

Fuel boilers with sturgeon then in plenty
removal of bodies for study
or something other
                        darkened the water with its schools

                        iron in the mountains
from algae from   photosynthetic cyanobacteria
their *great blooms* create an oxygen-atmosphere

rendering the mineral insoluble

sea   heaved into mountain range
rendering us

~

White birch burns in an Army-issue barrel-stove

dog sleeps behind desk
                              surrounded by beach rock
on windowsills   specimens from orogenies
or tectonic plate separation

                         magma surfaces & cools
becomes igneous   wears away into sediments
into sedimentary   a slow metamorphosis

a corruption of rock into language

Superior in light rain blurs into sky

~

Green frog startles from beach into water
swims quickly under the clear

⁓

Lamp-bright sleep   like a child
woods dark around me
                                    rocky headland ascent
north of camp   & a southern descent to shore

scramble to the crow's nest for sunset
& find it obscured by trees

without dog   a ruffed grouse barred & crested
I step further in & flush more from the branches

reconfigure this shore for the present
                        landscape-scale   blind to discontinuity

rock-persistence   bird-indicator
golden-crowned kinglet & yellow-bellied flycatcher

dog impatient   as I try to spot the chickadee
                                    I know is above too

warbler weight-gain slowed by neonicotinoids
cause delays in travel in

a review of intentions but not their consequences

~

Trace uranium found in the pitchblende
sources limited & mining short-lived

atom knowledge
distorts real & imagined

~

Ojibwe land   *gichi gami*

& another's before that

locate commonwealth in
sea & syllable

Sand everywhere   morning white pine mist
floating over point   ocean-sound

mined craters on overlook
                        highway noise through trees
pink-rock swirls overlayed
with moss lichen & pine needles   feldspar
makes red & epidote green

frog road-crossing
crow shredding carrion   blue jay flock emptying
burnt-red-brown fur on coyote dead roadside

The crystalline basement   vast lifeless ocean
with chains of volcanoes & volcanic islands
                                built up over thousands of eruptions

continental crusts of granite schist & gneiss
on my drive back lake & low clouds separated
in blackness by a thin mantle of coral-red

~

Orphan Lake hike to Superior cobble beach
waves receding sound like static over rock

~

Dog inspects
                              fish-head bobbing in foam

at Alona River's pebbled mouth

~

Pine needle in tea
dog curl

lichen   stone into green
no mechanism to filter

slow growing bioaccumulators

common-freckled-pelt smooth-rock-tripe & pitted-beard drape
as forest shifts from Great Lakes-St. Lawrence

to Boreal

to north

　　　～

We climb

past ancient lake terraces eroded & pitted
with intrusions from some later shifting

my position　　a shifting particle　　only known

through this measure　　tree sparrow scatter
on picnic table　　one immature golden plover
on the other side of the sandy river delta
a man fishes for salmon

another body to *operate the instrument*

　　　～

Red throated loon in Alona Bay   white & gray
I pick the solid gray stone fine-grained
a texture to obliterate decay

~

First night where the moon has shone
on water   making a bridge over waves as they break
over rock   drum of trucks passing

~

Asbestos fibers circulate Superior
from taconite tailings

~

Another fire before sun
star-remainder as I arrange wood   boil water
for coffee   *the line an altered forest*
unaccustomed to such blackness

Gray shimmering schist with a band of white quartz encircling
black crowns cone-clipped by squirrels
balsam fir pointing above

place-formation in movement

white-winged crossbills frantic feeding
in spruce over camp   sharp
chorus rattle

                    coiled carbonaceous
filaments two-feet long on bedding surfaces
spherical sporelike bodies two billion years old   carved in chert

Notebook corners grayed from ash on fingers
first juncos of season

A walk each day
power differentials

in dog step & boot slip

I insisted certain things about place & our position in it
an implication in the human geometry

Wake before light   moon sediment   stars
radial   areas of intense compression   folding
faulting heating   phenomena for making

woodsmoke-skin   rock-knowledge   home
daughter   settles the heaps of stones I've brought

~

BELLE ISLE

Across the Detroit River   peregrine
falcon steadies the *W*
of the Whittier Hotel on East Jefferson
translocal dispersal   common loon
in winter plumage   single blur crosshair
walking the ground of ourselves these
material bounds   expose   clefts
in known & whose share of

seawall collapse

On West Jefferson   aggregate pile
river-slip   Revere Copper &
Brass   uranium relict   residual
radiation   worrying   Fort Wayne
Windsor   Grosse Ile   *toxic colony*
a type of   matter over   man
is or is not the measure
of this *ghost ship* split

what recovery makes

Meaning for which species
winter wren snag   I saw it sing
near the handball courts
bramble low exposure & bristly
greenbrier   lines built through

unanticipated   merlin mistaken
for kestrel over kingfisher
on Blue Heron Lagoon

gadwall hidden within

Ring-necks & buffleheads
slow the car to watch a fox
devour a black-morphed gray squirrel
then trot into woods
semiotic turn   *destruction as investment*
as collateral for existence
grass carp European frogbit
or some yielding to

a similar sense of sameness

Leaf veins on wet ice
brown creeper branching   trio
of tree sparrows   rust-cast
concern-record   *dark garden*
in terms of multiples
carcass sloughed in amber sap
or field note scribble
black-duck sleep   out-sequencing

assemblies & symptoms

OXBOW

Styrofoam & roots define the strandline between
wet sand & dry grass   violence disguised in gradients
of green & gray   *countermodel to devastation*   I know
little bluestem & its purple autumn shock   redstart
canopy with tail feathers   this system for some
a type of reclamation   in between foredune & back
less wind & wave   *as glaciers remember heat*
the sea is changed   twig-rush bluejoint low calamint
fractal lake-coast   so many sets so

        sand black ridge
        magnetite & hematite

Where is order   sand-shapes from partial beached strides
between water & wrack   in morning without dog
two pileateds branched high across lagoon   *collective*
singularity   & *orders of magnitude* we can't begin
to decode   two sanderlings on the wet shore
black tail feathers black beaks & eyes   swerving
assembled on familiar terrain   eastern wood-pewee
calls day-long   note trails oak outside my cabin
where acorns drop like stones

        dead birch row
        from window

Muskrat skims canoe   ring-billed gulls scramble
over apple core on beach   *an animal among other animals*
horsemint flowers soft to touch   redtop spray
of small dark seeds & thin lines   a form of escapism
or *ecological embeddedness*   a type of *compulsive monitoring*
button bush   elm-seed scatter near milkweed
screen door banging shut   chicken drinking
from last night's puddles   filling small depressions
in the gravel path between cabins   tea mug steams

       green cottage squats
       on hills of sand

Circle of charred beachwood   once lighthouse
now trespass   my dream of her last night
memory as constructive agency   Kalamazoo River emptying
slowly over silt & shallow   until the mouth filled
with sand & sealed the passage into lake shut
two towns along oxbow-become-lagoon sand-buried
Blanchard's cricket frog sings metallic
vascularized skin absorbs waste more quickly than most
post-creature currency   thumb-nail frog-song

       dark triangle
       between the eyes

INTERDUNAL

Common greenshield lichen cut
into half-circle on firewood
fluted pale-paper lobes overlapping
jack pine sand   relic dune
sea rocket dispersed by
wind & wave as monarchs
glide south   migration
a liminal act

      lake-float

As I descend the first dune
marram grass   little blue
sand-reed   milkweed pod
green becoming red as
water table rises to wetland
two field sparrows   their soft
seep seep as they forage seed
gray eye crescent

      meadow-wet

Red boots soaked & plaited
with sand   I ascend
around a blowout   knowing
now how that looks   carved
crater where nothing grows
cottonwood on ridge   spotted-
knapweed & creeping juniper
endless interglacial

        open-orbit

Bird whistles fill canopy before
rain   current spins canoe
into sideways float   composition
by field or force   to know
what constitutes the *sensation*
of being   of the bodies of animal-
others engaged in somatic
forms of living

        lagoon-rift

De-inking process becomes
dam to lake   80 miles of
Superfund   papermill towns
persist in cubic yards of PCBs
blue-headed vireo probes
spider web   *interim actions*
only removed by classification
by dredge & bury

      river-mirage

Heron circling before landing
a kind of *double awareness*
like river currents carrying
lumber effluent *operable units*
purple sandpiper harlequin duck
act of presentness in finite &
flight   in record & riparian
social practice &

      sandy-loam

BESTIARY

Ghost moose in dark coniferous woods
pale beast wanders through downed needles
trading grass for tick   by warmer winters & less
snow fall   a type of *two-eyed seeing* or *ecological memory*
wolf whitens into age in a field of stones
permanent infidel   primitive dream becoming
one type of *evolutionary chimera*   I see
the forms fermenting in darkness
candle & lamp-wick from milkweed

      mollusk memory
      adaptive radiation

      ~

Spectacular dominance   common ancestors & pre-human
collateral lines   one more fortunate turn into
the generative maze   *cut marks found on a fossil antelope bone*
we were specialists in group selection   in daily life
of one kind of subsistence or another   ice-house
gas-house   barter white for blue for
paper   rain   lake   sand   sawdust-tailings
the porcupine's phosphorescent quills on my morning walk
in the time between climatic shifts   a burgeoning

      king rail emerges
      from high grass

Cowbird's mottled eggs buried beneath layers
of yellow warbler nests   shadow from the cold
pine-moon   chronically yellow-white   I trace
the edge with my finger   starved voyageurs
eating rock-tripe lichen   collecting bounty
for predator   a savage engagement to delay
the onset of the next age   positive feedbacks accelerate
consensus as a means   her face in my dream ringed
weight of evidence   collected in dark

      red squirrel
      guards seed-cache

      ~

A system of interlocking tribes   ash-mountain
bone-refuse   we snowshoe across the tapered point
of Pelee Island in gray-blue February
under blue-white cloud cover   a few reflect
sunlight back to the origin   *albedo* &
the ice also   glinting raft of canvasbacks
& glaucous gulls on near-frozen Lake Erie
in blue-drifts migrants dip under for rhizome & larvae
autocatalytic each turn makes the next

      spectacled eider
      on pack ice

BLUE

Cardinal flashes his black mask
at the bird bath   lost in waves
& winter air   *densely clustered floes* break up
north of here   ice branches like tree limbs
on the window's transparent landscape
on this cold day spent at home
the scale & the speed *marked by*
golden spikes in the record like *volcano*
or *meteor* or *acidification*   the wild twigs
the *husks of trees*

       middle life
       marked
       by *conodont*

We gather beneath the Blue Water Bridge
to glimpse a peregrine falcon where the mouth
of Lake Huron narrows into St. Clair River's ice
breakers & floes   *the sky draws down its fog*
over a bevy of long-tailed ducks   winter visitors
from northern edges   black arrows
bob & dive   snow covers the *lean & hungry*
sand only fit for pines   single bufflehead
diminished by barrens of canvasbacks
& redheads on gray waves

      snowy owl
      green buoy
      perch

St. John's Marsh enveloped by phragmites   tall seed-
heads sway in bitter air   storing their mass
beneath   *when the cups are empty*
a black rail   dark little gnome   a black tern
dark-head on gray breast   biological
desert   *but I in my weakness deserted that which was once*
occurring   on sand ridges overlaid with clay
blazing-stars & bluebills   Atlantic & Mississippi
flyways merge near western Lake Erie
a corridor for now

     broken bulrush
     makeshift-
     colony

I ought to begin another I thought   unhinge
the limitation of bodies   skin tide
waiting for spring at Seney Refuge
Le Conte's sparrow sedge-wren Cape May
warbler in black spruce   ruddy turnstone
at Whitefish Point   last year four wolves
were brought to Isle Royale   in February one female
crossed the ice-bridge   fourteen miles back home
her leavetaking   a lean figure
knocking the order off

          beak-flipped stones
          crustacean
          staccato

          ⁓

Red-bellied woodpecker on roof   sliver
of sun on desk   search the amber
for a revelation   *a potent cultural relict   pressed*
into fine-grained rock   geese overhead
break formation to slow their speed
before landing on water   altered beyond
recognition   I look for my daughter's face
in the window   drink cold tea
recall the map the dog's prints made
in new snow this morning as she ran

blue-
spectrum
from white

~

JANUARY

January ice-walk around Carpenter Lake   dog & daughter
slide out onto the ice   I worry over them *& the blue surrounding*
she tosses her walking stick onto the frozen surface
watches it skitter over the white   *the sea is mine* she says
one goldeneye in a constellation of mallards
beneath the bridge two mute swans sleep on ice
heads wing-tucked   some *wilder forms on troubled ground*
leaf trapped roadside beneath a thin layer of icy-mud
I break it open with my boot & search the pines
for the scatter of crows   screaming & mobbing
a short-eared owl   until it's forced into the clearing

     black noise
     empty bough
     rattle

Cold half-oak moon outside our winter window
small collapse of climate when the original inhabitants
all died   the forest returned & a cooling came
a crane gleaning a snail from sand   *evolution linked*
to favorable temperatures   irruption of winter finches
pine-grosbeak redpoll white-winged-crossbills blink red
& white in backyard drifts   *stones rattling onwards in their course*
cone & birch seeds   daughter treks through banks & steeps
of frozen clouds   less ice & more rain for now
snowshoe trail into woods   black dog buries
her paws in white snow   fine freckling warms to wet

       mountain-ash frenzy
       faint warbling
       tea

       ~

Daughter dressed in layers to venture out into the white
her winter strata   pavement too cold for dog's rough pads
solid bodies within solids persist in the vein   sea creatures
as seen by rock-cutters   *human* as geological force
the remains of that sky   piece of the polar vortex
fallen into Michigan   wind-bands near the north pole break
daughter draws a mountain & a tree   places an outsized
version of herself next to each   *a hierarchical series*
of ever finer slices   snow outside glows blue & gray as we watch
a red-tailed hawk on the neighbor's concrete steps
tear apart a rabbit   gray fur floating on arctic breeze

     dark band
     edges
     cinnamon tail

ICE

We search snow-covered fields for snowy owls
& come up empty   white empty   snow geese overhead
sail of black beneath white wings   crooked cabin
on ice-rimmed Lake Michigan   night falls
lake & sky a *braid of bodies*   ice here
a *needle of light*   before a storm

Snowshoe treads on Old Baldy   lichen on bark
expands in circles   pale-green brown & gray
woodpecker-bored snags & chickadees at the edges
frame of mine   made of fluted points   language gathers ice
nowhere permanent   threshold of complexity for
working memory   most perishable of artifacts

What the black gown has said   slipping the net
no sense of urgency at the beginning   only sequence
of ice-mountains near shore   white path
as sun dips beneath horizon   this *string of*
illumination   pushed them into a new
theory of mind   snowfall overnight

I sleep next to the fire   splintered glow
single hairy woodpecker in the woods today
steady drill sounding in the quiet
if I made it to the end
I would see the lake's shape snake into dimness
& then fall away

Ice crystal stars spread in six directions along the surface
dilating beehive sheets   *becalmed in white space*
flowing under its own weight
lake still in morning & churning at dusk
around ice   we drink our tea
birds line the wind like a row of pebbles

Ancient ice-keel scours where icebergs plowed
through sea beds   curvilinear troughs & sub-circular
patterns   raked garden   submerged
same ridges found on now lifeless planets
where there once was water   white slurry turning
transparent   then gray & finally to dust

LAKE

Red-tiered purple martin house on lake's fringe
the *binding effects*   the *emergent traits*   a single *allele*
separating *now* from *before*   or rather *us* from *them*
a wetland is a spawning ground   for musky for northern pike
& deepwater sculpin   depth-dweller
mottled gray & brown   once thought extirpated from
eutrophication   from Erie & Ontario   water floods & retreats
pintails & blue-winged teals search shallows for shoots
of duckweed or water plantain   *a problem of alliances* I told her
but this does not mean an absence of social order
a body turning into bone or wind   black-crowned
night-heron & least bittern shelter among the reeds
the heart of   a *dense immateriality*

      sora roams
      muddy edge
      tail flicking

A once unnamed sea   ice sheets move like *slow beasts*
vertical front   brittle cavity   large fracture
as winter withdraws   we count white-throated sparrow
fox sparrow   red & white nuthatches   red-bellied & downy
a well-formulated body of ideas & practices   when we read
we talked of cruelty   the male northern leopard frog
developing eggs after atrazine exposure   *a chemical castration*
daughter puts out eggshells for the martins
grit for digesting insect exoskeletons
every small part collected   spring-drift   lake-shift
glossy-blue   to plunder all in our *world of signs*
underwater the heron's legs like plant stems
as it hunts cricket frogs   black plumes trailing

                snow-melt peepers
                callout
                warm nights

                ~

Evolution is always occurring   a matter of
group selection *within a vast hereditary code*
the heron's s-shaped neck in flight   black feet tucked
tightly behind   each year hundreds of thousands
of pounds harvested until the blue walleye is
declared extinct   1985   later taxon rendered
invalid   only a morph of the yellow pike   *resting bodies*
bog buckbean used as a poultice once   daughter slips
into my bed in the morning   warm legs intertwine mine
some amphibians only return to their natal ponds
once a year   most of their lives spent in woods
beneath leaf-litter or high in the canopy
a phantom construction easily violated

     wood duck
     searches trees
     for acorns

Snapping turtle waits at lake bottom for crayfish
pointed snout   neck covered in blunt tubercles
hooked-beak strike sucks in prey   concentration
of PCBs makes eggs into decoys   *lake light*
preference for margins   language swells
to encompass   *paragraph   polychlorinated biphenyls*
puddle   downpour at dusk   little telegram
from dust   mallards dance on wet ground
summoning earthworms   green-headed patter
gene-culture coevolution & niche construction
throws our story into confusion   human nature as
a fixed property   philopatric defense   a still lake for now
collateral relationships   & string fens studded with cedars

        tree leafing
        with black
        crows

GRAY

I walk my black dog in sleet turned rain
gray blears into gray   white-winged scoter
skims   far from pelagic   white suns on dark face
Huron River   mussel & razor clam
dead goose bobs at lagoon edge   transfer sphere
of contention to new ground   substitute
race for class after arrival   *abstract the rules*
of equivalence   natural points funnel
disappeared prothonotary warbler   perimeter
narrows for bobwhite & bobolink   accounts of
stripped-assets   & leaves & divisions

      known from form
      form from

Traces   named *Orbis Spike*   a dip in carbon
after reforestation after *Columbian Exchange* after 50 million
perish   disease & slaughter   lake sediment
cave stalagmite samples   *who moved upon the Sea*
let loose by Night   snow melt from roof
a slow steady drip   *life as a march of*   as more than
human   as darkness *let loose by Morning*   prey caught
on the wing   chimney swift whip-poor-will
systemic insecticides across scales & waterways
intersectional paradigm as seed coating   we leave
remainders in the formation of something else

                blackfin cisco
                piping plover

On beachwood   sand-colored bodies go unnoticed
on sandy shores   forage snail & water beetle
basins threaded into new Pangea   routes replace
plate tectonics as a culling force   I gather my daughter
outside the school doors   enclosures *obfuscate the thinking*
of men   sing the name of frog fugue fog   to inhabit
is to *lay order upon the long sky*   words as mountains
worn down to roundness   as tracks on a map
that favors power in its design   one way
to chronicle what was shipped back
over the sea & back   making of two

                an other &
                its value

Extended to some   *places that lie between two states*
neither disoriented nor settled   a material turn
lichen life in the margins   drift   fret   threat
breaker of   before feels so long   a time when
desocialize the territory   ease the guilt of perpetuators
map the cultural system   we watch the jays & grackles
come & go   blue alight on spring   half-animal
half-blaze   single eastern bluebird flutters woods
the singular reigns & is all   panopticon

can be seen in figure   wake to snow-cover
all-human   a trace in the geography

      make trail
      as track

Make track as time   snow-surface unbroken in blue
all-home   late March skunk cabbage
emergent in cold soil   locate spring
in tendril tender   loggerhead shrike
hunts arthropod & rodent in unplanted fields
domination without subject   yellow-bellied sapsucker's
high stuttered dream   *evidence of concealing power*
watch jay discard peanut shells from wire
star rubble   window lit against *the long float*
toward land   I trace you   ice between cells
wood frog's duck-song echoes

through leafless
trees

MIGRATION

What world from waves & stones
attention to inhabit   space as gasp
this season   migration home-bound
I walk the chipped path   apart
we find them   some comfort to see

      year after year

Placement-remember   yellowthroat
northern parula   *a total sharing of identities*
blue-back yellow-chest   sweet ascent
Baltimore orioles high as trees leaf
systems at play   my catalogue

      of not

Feather   text-scatter   *primitive
memory   culture-detritus*   I mark the edge
where I gaze   Acadian flycatcher
only differentiated by sound
what if I claim this map in waxwing mask

      & berry blaze

Red pretend   immortal materials remake
our perception of time   scarlet tanager
in the highest   *changes in degree become*
changes in kind   house in the ferns
snapping turtles burrowed

      sandy-roadside

We look for them   across the Platte River
wood-rise   *multiple temporalities* in a single frame
pressure-creator   joy swallowtail buzz
lines of movement like lead shot
we say *shot through*

      with contact

Saw-whet breeding linked to mouse
or vole   to slow walks & long ago
dark jay in tree   dusk-shape
interstitial skitter   we hike Proud Lake
& hear spring peepers   wood &

      chorus frogs

Daughter probes decaying trunk
with dead branch   early bluebird & phoebe
goldfinch-morph *brings sun from cold's bloom*
less oxygen in the water column
each season   springfish die-off

      liminal float

I note Magnolia Nashville Tennessee
kingbird green heron   May 6th ground-
truthed   craggy spaced   we write
soft pandemonium   three sparrows & two
swallows   song Lincoln's white-throated

      leaves ramshackle

Late spring sleet then sun   walk is
only one type of   house-making   when
a system is cut off   we think we glimpse a Kirtland's
one morning on our same path   wood-break
migrants frequent its edges   spatial practice

      drastically collective

Daughter trek to Lake St. Clair   carp-thrash
great horned owlets in a fork-perched
metal washtub   fox snake   grosbeak
my notes mark species & little else   only marking
without   I wrote *rescale attention to the rough*

    biotic periphery

We saw the yellow warbler on her nest
flimsy cup from grass & web   daughter finds me
with her good morning   I stop
& walk with her   red-spotted purples
in road   one spiny snapper near bridge

    mossy shell

Bladder campion in woods   meadow ferns &
oxeye daisies   wild geranium's star-cut leaves
sail shaped shade over porch   *dismantled of time*
gun-shots in distance   in the noise
of birds   interleaves of relation

    for now

Notes

On nature, climate, & science: *Meeting the Universe Halfway: Quantum Physics and the Entanglement of Matter and Meaning*, Karen Barad; *The Human Planet: How We Created the Anthropocene*, Simon L. Lewis and Mark A. Maslin; *The End of the Wild*, Stephen M. Meyer; *Water: A Natural History*, Alice B. Outwater; *Environmental Culture*, Val Plumwood; *A Farewell to Ice: A Report from the Arctic*, Peter Wadhams; and Edward O. Wilson's trilogy *The Social Conquest of Earth, The Meaning of Human Existence,* and *Half-Earth: Our Planet's Fight for Life.*

On early North American history: *The Nature of Empire and the Empires of Nature: Indigenous Peoples and The Great Lakes Environment*, Karl S. Hele; *Regeneration Through Violence: The Mythology of the American Frontier*, Richard Slotkin; and *The Middle Ground: Indians, Empires, and Republics in the Great Lakes Region*, Richard White.

On the Great Lakes Basin: *The Late, Great Lakes: An Environmental History*, Williams Ashworth; *Around the Shores of Lake Superior*, Margaret Bogue; *The Living Great Lakes: Searching for the Heart of the Inland Seas*, Jerry Dennis; *The Great Lakes: The Natural History of a Changing Region*, Wayne Grady; *Ancient Life of the Great Lakes Basin: Precambrian to Pleistocene*, J. Alan Holman; *Geology of the Lake Superior Region*, Gene L. LaBerge; *Walking Paths and Protected Areas of the Keweenaw*, Nancy Leonard; and various field guides on birds, lichens, trees, amphibians and reptiles, mammals, butterflies, rocks and minerals, wildflowers, and coastal plants.

On poetry, ecopoetics, and language: *Writing and Difference*, Jacque Derrida; *The Great Derangement: Climate Change and the Unthinkable*, Amitav Ghosh; *Eco Language Reader*, Brenda Iijima; *The Small Space of a Pause: Susan Howe's Poetry and The Space Between*, Elisabeth W. Joyce; *Recomposing Ecopoetics: North American Poetry of the Self-Conscious Anthropocene*, Lynn Keller; *The Poethical Wager* and "What is Experimental

Poetry and Why Do We Need It," Joan Retallack; and *Anthropocene Poetics: Deep Time, Sacrifice Zones, and Extinction,* David Farrier.

The composition of these poems coincided with my travels around the Great Lakes Region, often alone, sometimes with my dog, daughter, or husband, in one combination or another. My traveling poetics was inspired by Lorine Niedecker's 1966 circumnavigation of Lake Superior and the Wave Books edition *Superior.* And also, Kobayashi Yataro's (pen-name Issa, which means "a cup of tea") haibun form in *The Year of My Life,* and his attention to the smallest and lowliest creatures on Earth.

The poems are in conversation with my place-based treks, with texts about those places, and with other poets, writers, thinkers, through their language. Much of the borrowed text in the poems is from the sources noted above. Other collage fragments are acknowledged below.

North: *the smell of the lake follows me inland*, Nathaniel Farrell; *my canoe seemed as if it hung suspended*, Jonathan Carver; *creative destruction*, John Schumpeter; *so that we alone can live* and *night descends*, Giovanni Singleton; and *drift and slip of a body*, Juliet Patterson.

Spring: *ever darker territory*, David Wallace Wells; and *words like chromosomes*, Inger Christensen.

Migration: *us out of ourselves*, Arthur Sze; and *belief in registers (original: "believes in registers")*, Yanyi.

Pointe Mouillee: *an endless dark corridor*, Henry Gee.

~

Rabbit Bay: *one world leading into another (original: "one world leads into another without introduction")*, Sally Keith; *our own animal feelings*, Derrick Jensen; and *unmade as resource*, Elizabeth Robinson.

Sea: *heaped in thin* and *slain marked O*, Susan Howe.

Upper Peninsula: *structures of perception*, Forrest Gander.

Keweenaw: *watch ourselves cross the dark*, Monica Berlin and Beth Marzoni; *black pocket of memory (original: "black pocket we call memory")*, Holly Amos; *sometimes a bird sometimes a stone (original: "sometimes the man felt like the bird and sometimes the man felt like a stone")*, Richard Siken; and *water that touched shore so long ago*, Brian Teare.

Superior: *a service on the surface, experiment with beginning,* and *claim catastrophe,* Fred Moten; and *I keep repeating,* C. Violet Eaton.

~

Theano Point: *a corruption of rock into language (original: "glorious corruption of rock and language"),* Lorine Niedecker; and *the line an altered forest (original: "the line/is always quietly an altered forest"),* Cole Swensen.

~

Belle Isle: *ghost ship* and *destruction as investment,* Ed Roberson.

Interdunal: *sensation of being,* J.M. Coetzee.

Oxbow: *as glaciers remember heat,* Juliana Spahr; and *collective singularity,* Forrest Gander.

Blue: *husks of trees,* Mary Oliver; *the sky draws down its fog,* Rusty Morrison; *when the cups are empty* and *but I in my weakness,* Issa; *the limitation of bodies,* Ada Limón; and *skin tide,* Margaret Yocom.

Bestiary: *forms fermenting in darkness (original: "let my writing ferment in darkness"),* Tiana Clark.

~

January: *the sea is mine,* Jack Collum; *the blue surrounding,* Marianne Moore; *troubled ground,* Brian Teare; *stones rattling onwards in their course,* Charles Darwin; and *the remains of that sky,* Susan Gevirtz.

Ice: *needle of light,* Marianne Boruch; *frame of mine* and *nowhere permanent,* Basho; and *becalmed in white space,* Thomas A. Clark.

Lake: *dense immateriality,* Rusty Morrison; and *world of signs,* Susan Howe.

Gray: *obfuscate the thinking of men,* S.W. Boggs via Jena Osman; *evidence of concealing power,* Adam Fagin; and *the long float toward land,* Adam Clay.

Migration: *changes in degree become changes in kind,* Donna Haraway; *brings sun from cold's bloom,* Leslie Harrison; and *dismantled of time,* Henry Wei Leung.

Acknowledgments

This book wouldn't have surfaced without the support of my husband Matt and our travels around our newish home-state of Michigan with our daughter Lucy and our dog Katie. Katie, a medium-sized black and white pit-mix rescue, accompanied me to numerous remote locations and was my sole companion for weeks at a time. Thank you to Susan Tichy for her guidance on this project and our weekly correspondence about birds and words. And for Rick Ledoux, who introduced me to birding in Michigan. Thank you to Adam Clay for my first invitation to visit the Keweenaw Peninsula. On a trip to the Keweenaw later that same year, I met, or rather Katie, my dog, met Kerrie Richert and Bryce Holden, which led to many more visits—filled with hikes, sauna sessions, stories, games of cribbage, and sunsets over Superior.

I am grateful to Steve and Robin Read for making my time away more possible and for Matt, Jaquie, Elliot, Caz, and Ezra Zeman, my far-away family. Thank you to Kay Smalley at Ox-Bow for speaking with me about her life with the flora and fauna there.

Lisa Ampleman, Renee Angle, Jess Anthony, and Courtney Campbell each read and provided feedback on these poems. I spent a week at The Wild in Ontario on a remote Lake Superior bay thanks to Jocelyn Clair Burke and two weeks in a cabin at Ox-Bow School of Art and Artists' Residency on Lake Michigan, also. Revision accommodations were generously provided by Katherine and Mike DiClaudio at their cottage "up north."

Thank you to Jon Thompson and David Blakesly at Parlor Press for selecting and publishing this book.

Finally, thank you to the following journals for publishing my work:

> *About Place Journal,* "Belle Isle";
> *Annulet,* "Theano Point," "Spring," and "Pointe Mouillee";

Bracken, "Lake";
Conduit, "Superior";
Denver Quarterly, "Migration," "Interdunal," and "Ice";
Mississippi Review, "Keweenaw";
Permafrost, "Upper Peninsula";
Rhino, "Oxbow";
Under a Warm Green Linden, "Sea";
& *VOLT,* "Blue," and "Gray."

About the Author

Writing at the intersection of ecology and culture, habitat and habitation, Tracy Zeman's work traverses environmental crises, witnesses disappearing species, and mediates the moral and ethical implications of this age of ecological unraveling. Her first collection of poetry, *Empire* (2020, Parlor Press) won the New Measure Poetry Prize. Her poems have been published in *Chicago Review, Denver Quarterly, VOLT*, and others, and her essays and book reviews have appeared in journals such as *Annulet, Kenyon Review, The Cincinnati Review*, and *Colorado Review*. She has earned residencies from the Sitka Center for Art and Ecology, Ox-Bow School of Art and Artist Residency, The Wild, and Write On Door County. In fall 2022, she spent two weeks off the grid as an artist-in-residence in nonfiction on remote Isle Royale, a National Park in Lake Superior. She teaches at the University of Michigan and lives outside Detroit, Michigan, with her husband, daughter, and dog, where she hikes and bird watches in all seasons.

Photograph of the author by
Kyle Rollins. Used by permission.

Free Verse Editions

Edited by Jon Thompson

13 ways of happily by Emily Carr
& in Open, Marvel by Felicia Zamora
& there's you still thrill hour of the world to love by Aby Kaupang
Alias by Eric Pankey
the atmosphere is not a perfume it is odorless by Matthew Cooperman
At Your Feet (A Teus Pés) by Ana Cristina César, edited by
    Katrina Dodson, trans. by Brenda Hillman and Helen Hillman
Bari's Love Song by Kang Eun-Gyo, translated by Chung Eun-Gwi
Between the Twilight and the Sky by Jennie Neighbors
Blade Work by Lily Brown
Blood Orbits by Ger Killeen
The Bodies by Christopher Sindt
The Book of Isaac by Aidan Semmens
The Calling by Bruce Bond
Canticle of the Night Path by Jennifer Atkinson
Child in the Road by Cindy Savett
Civil Twilight by Giles Goodland
Condominium of the Flesh by Valerio Magrelli, trans. by Clarissa Botsford
Contrapuntal by Christopher Kondrich
Country Album by James Capozzi
Cry Baby Mystic by Daniel Tiffany
The Curiosities by Brittany Perham
Current by Lisa Fishman
Day In, Day Out by Simon Smith
Dear Reader by Bruce Bond
Dismantling the Angel by Eric Pankey
Divination Machine by F. Daniel Rzicznek
Elsewhere, That Small by Monica Berlin
Empire by Tracy Zeman
Erros by Morgan Lucas Schuldt
Extinction of the Holy City by Bronisław Maj, trans. by Daniel Bourne
Field Notes of a Flaneur by Lewis Meyers
Fifteen Seconds without Sorrow by Shim Bo-Seon, trans. by
    Chung Eun-Gwi and Brother Anthony of Taizé
The Forever Notes by Ethel Rackin
The Flying House by Dawn-Michelle Baude
General Release from the Beginning of the World by Donna Spruijt-Metz

Spine by Carolyn Guinzio
Spool by Matthew Cooperman
Strange Antlers by Richard Jarrette
A Suit of Paper Feathers by Nate Duke
Summoned by Guillevic, trans. by Monique Chefdor & Stella Harvey
Sunshine Wound by L. S. Klatt
System and Population by Christopher Sindt
There Are as Many Songs in the World as Branches of Coral by
     Elizabeth Jacobson
These Beautiful Limits by Thomas Lisk
They Who Saw the Deep by Geraldine Monk
The Thinking Eye by Jennifer Atkinson
This History That Just Happened by Hannah Craig
An Unchanging Blue: Selected Poems 1962–1975 by
     Rolf Dieter Brinkmann, trans. by Mark Terrill
Under the Quick by Molly Bendall
Verge by Morgan Lucas Schuldt
The Visible Woman by Allison Funk
The Wash by Adam Clay
Well by Sasha Steensen
We'll See by Georges Godeau, trans. by Kathleen McGookey
What Stillness Illuminated by Yermiyahu Ahron Taub
Winter Journey [Viaggio d'inverno] by Attilio Bertolucci, trans. by
     Nicholas Benson
Wonder Rooms by Allison Funk

www.ingramcontent.com/pod-product-compliance
Lightning Source LLC
Chambersburg PA
CBHW031143090426
42738CB00008B/1203